Published by Writers' Workshops International, LLC
San Rafael, California, USA 94903.
www.writersworskhopsinternational.com

Book design by Pete Masterson, Æonix Publishing Group, www.aeonix.com.
Text set in ITC Souvenir.

Publisher's Cataloguing-in-Publication Data

Euser, Barbara J.
   The neighbor and the stone : a modern Greek fable
/ Barbara J. Euser   illustrated by Jim DeWitt.
      p. cm.
      Summary: In the Greek countryside, a misunderstanding which arises
      between neighbors is creatively resolved.

   ISBN 978-0-9842992-1-8

1. Greece-Fiction. 2. Folk tales-Fiction. 3. Neighbors-Fiction. 4. Dispute
resolution. 5. Problem solving. 6. Cooperation.
I. DeWitt, Jim, ill. II. Title.

WRITERS' WORKSHOPS
INTERNATIONAL

Printed in Singapore

The Neighbor
and the Stone

A Modern Greek Fable

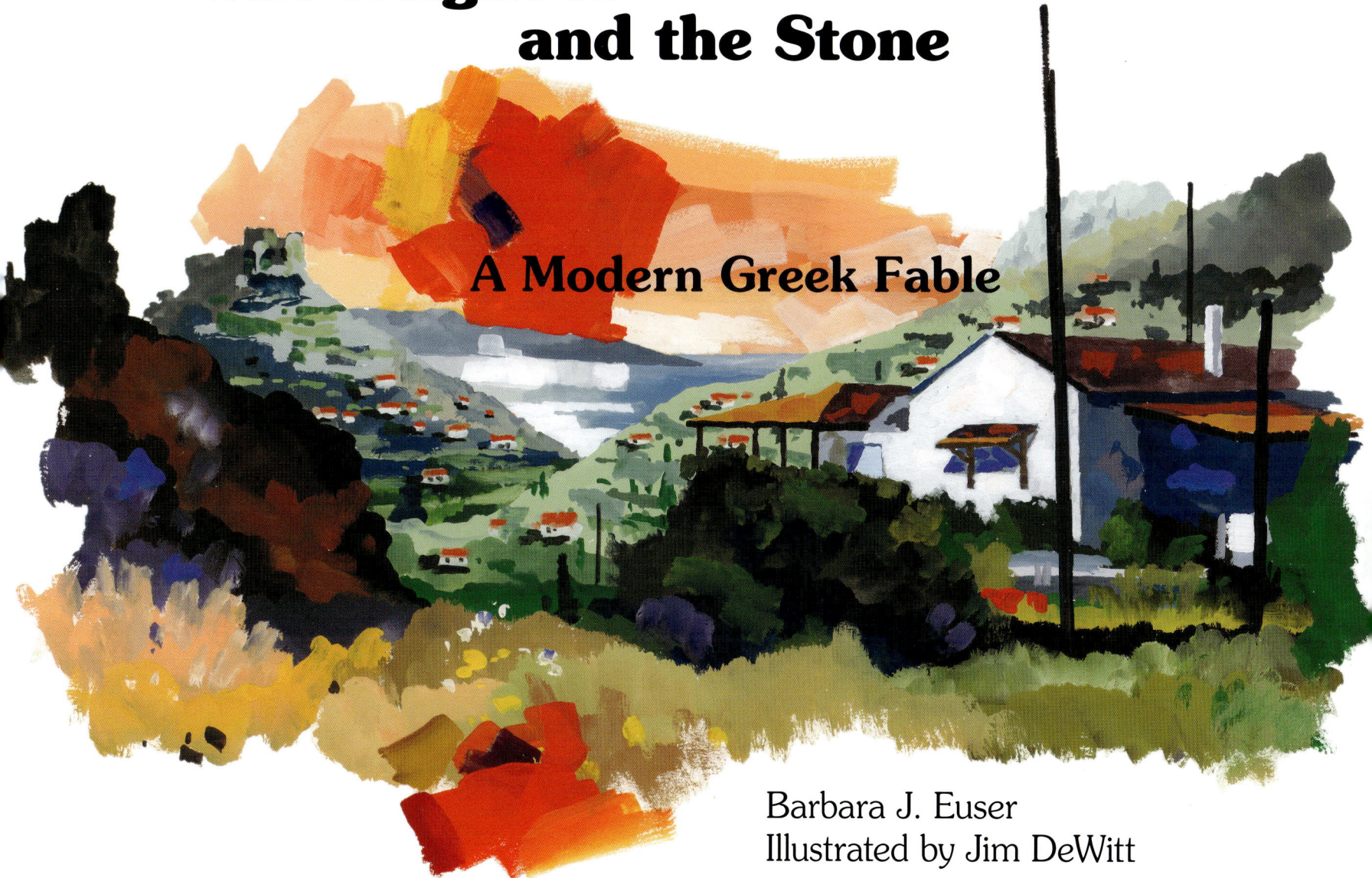

Barbara J. Euser
Illustrated by Jim DeWitt

To Sallie – J.D.

To Helane and Piper – B.J.E.

On the side of the mountain outside a small town in the south of Greece, lived a woman in a white house with a red tile roof. Her house was like all white houses with red tile roofs in that part of Greece. Her name was Chrysoula.

One day an American woman bought the farm next to Chrysoula's. The American woman's name was Virginia.

The farms on the mountainside were built with stone terraces. The terraces made flat ground for olive trees to grow.

The stone terraces on Virginia's farm needed repair.

Virginia hired a stone mason
to repair the terraces. The
stone mason brought his wife
to help him with his work.

The work went well. But as the stone mason finished the terrace wall, he found he needed one more stone, just the size of a loaf of bread.

"Will you find me a stone the size of a loaf of bread?" the stone mason asked his wife.

The stone mason's wife began
searching the ground for just the
right stone. She wandered off of
Virginia's farm onto Chrysoula's
farm. She saw a stone just the size
of a loaf of bread. She picked up
the stone and started to carry it to
her husband.

"Stop!" cried Chrysoula. "What do you think you are doing? You are stealing my stone."

Surprised and ashamed, the stone mason's wife dropped the stone. She hurried back to where her husband was working.

She searched for a stone in the opposite direction. Soon she found another stone just the size of a loaf of bread.

She carried it back to her husband. He placed it in the terrace wall. The wall was complete.

Later, Virginia searched
her own farm for stones
the size of a loaf of bread.
She picked up ten stones.
She put them in her
wheelbarrow.

She wheeled her wheelbarrow
up the driveway of her neighbor
Chrysoula's house.

"What are you doing?" Chrysoula asked. "Why are you bringing me a wheelbarrow full of stones?"

"We are neighbors. I want to be a good neighbor to you. I heard my worker took a stone from you. I want to repay you for that stone with not just one stone, but with ten stones," Virginia replied.

"But I don't need ten stones," Chrysoula objected. "I have too many stones already on my farm. I do not want ten stones. I do not want to have to pay someone to carry them away."

"All right," Virginia agreed. "My stones can stay in my
wheelbarrow. But please pick one stone out of the ten.

That stone is for the top of the low wall between our properties.

"It will remind us that having a good neighbor is more important than any stone."

BARBARA J. EUSER is a former political officer with the Foreign Service of the U.S. Department of State. Her articles and essays have appeared in newspapers, magazines and anthologies. She is the author and editor of ten books. Barbara met Jim DeWitt at the Richmond Yacht Club, of which they both are members. She owns an olive farm in the southern Peloponnese in Greece, where she produces organic olive oil and writes.

JIM DEWITT was born in Oakland, California, in 1930.

As a five-year-old, he drew pictures of the sailboat his father was building in their backyard, and dreamed of someday being her skipper. After high school, he studied art for six years at the California College of Arts and Crafts and Los Angeles Art Center — learning sailmaking and racing sailboats in his spare time.

In addition to shows and exhibitions in San Diego, San Francisco, New York, Waikiki and Newport, Rhode Island, Jim has exhibited in galleries and museums worldwide. Jim's racing paintings are valued assets in private and corporate collections, and are on permanent display in many yacht clubs.

Today, Jim is happiest painting colorful, joyful subject matter that tells a story. His work can be seen on his website, www.jimdewitt.com and at DeWitt Gallery and Framing in Point Richmond, California.